MW00791340

On-the-Go
Prayers

On-the-Go Prayers

One-Minute Prayers for Busy Families

Susan K. Leigh

CONCORDIA PUBLISHING HOUSE • SAINT LOUIS

May the God of hope fill you with all joy
and peace in believing, so that by
the power of the Holy Spirit
you may abound in hope.

Romans 15:13

This book is a gift to

_____

From

_____

Date

_____

For Jack and Kendall and Sophie and Sam.

Table of Contents

Introduction

Rejoice always, pray without ceasing,
give thanks in all circumstances;
for this is the will of God in
Christ Jesus for you.

1 Thessalonians 5:16–18

One of my good friends says short "thank You, Jesus" prayers continually throughout her day. She doesn't miss a beat. Every little thing and big thing in her life is lifted up in prayer. When I first learned of her practice, I was delighted by her faith and, I confess, chagrined that I didn't have the same kind of prayer life. To be sure, I have had the habit of regular bedtime prayer since I was a very young child. I pray when I'm troubled, when I'm happy, and for others who are in need. I rejoice in the opportunity to join with my brothers and sisters in Christ in corporate prayer during the worship service. But until that long-ago conversation with my friend, I seldom thought to pray before I set out on my daily commute, for example, or when I arrived home at the end of the day.

The inspiration for this particular collection of prayers came from yet another friend who told me that she and her daughters pray in the car before beginning the drive to school and work every morning. Such a practice is a beautiful exercise in spiritual discipline and an example of faithful parenting. I had her family in mind as I thought about the occasions for the prayers contained in this book. Therefore, some prayers here are specific to situations and events common to school-age children and are intended to be read by them. Other prayers are intended to be said by the parent with the child and are more general in nature. The prayers on pages 17–23 are traditional Christian prayers and will be familiar to people of all ages.

Prayer is a gift. God invites us to pray to Him about everything, and He promises that He hears all prayers in Jesus' name. We pray to our heavenly Father with confidence because we know that Jesus Himself reconciled us to Him and intercedes on our behalf. Therefore, we know that God answers our prayers with a yes, no, or wait, for He has something better in mind for us.

Prayer is a responsibility. God calls parents to pray for their children and to teach them about prayer, what it is, and why we do it. This is one way that parents model spiritual discipline and faith that God hears our prayers in Jesus' name.

Prayer is a joy. It helps us keep our hearts and minds centered in God, and it reminds us to keep God's will in front of us. Because Jesus is our Redeemer, we can be sure that God is pleased by our conversation with Him and loves to hear our prayers.

The prayers offered here are deliberately short so they can be incorporated into the family's busy daily routines. I suggest that you keep this book in plain sight and easy reach so you and your children can turn to it often. Perhaps you'll even want to keep it in your car to use as part of your last-minute preparations before you leave home. My hope is it helps you make prayer one of the final things you do as you make your way out the door at the beginning of the day and one of the first things you do when you return home.

However it benefits you, my intention for this book is that it would encourage parents and children to pray at all times and in all places. Then, regardless of what known and unknown things await us, we can go forth

with peace in our hearts, knowing that our Lord God
is faithful to us in Christ Jesus.

> Do not be anxious about anything, but
> in everything by prayer and supplication
> with thanksgiving let your requests be
> made known to God.
>
> Philippians 4:6

The Author
Holy Week, 2013

Classic Prayers

Lord's Prayer

Our Father, who art in heaven, hallowed be Thy name, Thy kingdom come, Thy will be done on earth as it is in heaven. Give us this day our daily bread; and forgive us our trespasses as we forgive those who trespass against us; and lead us not into temptation, but deliver us from evil. For Thine is the kingdom and the power and the glory forever and ever. Amen.

Morning Prayer

I thank You, my heavenly Father, through Jesus Christ, Your dear Son, that You have kept me this night from all harm and danger; and I pray that You would keep me this day also from sin and every evil, that all my doings and life may please You. For into Your hands I commend myself, my body and soul, and all things. Let Your holy angel be with me, that the evil foe may have no power over me. Amen.

(Luther's Small Catechism)

Evening Prayer

I thank You, my heavenly Father, through Jesus Christ, Your dear Son, that You have graciously kept me this day; and I pray that You would forgive me all my sins where I have done wrong, and graciously keep me this night. For into Your hands I commend myself, my body and soul, and all things. Let Your holy angel be with me, that the evil foe may have no power over me. Amen.

(Luther's Small Catechism)

We thank You, Lord God, heavenly Father, for all Your benefits, through Jesus Christ, our Lord, who lives and reigns with You and the Holy Spirit forever and ever. Amen.

(Luther's Small Catechism, Returning Thanks)

Heavenly Father, hear our prayer;
Keep us in Your loving care.
Guard us through the coming day
In our work and in our play.
Keep us pure and strong and true;
Help us, Lord, Your will to do. Amen.

(Adapted from *Little Folded Hands*, p. 8)

For this new morning and its light,
For rest and shelter of the night,
For health and food, for love and
    friends,
For everything Your goodness sends
I thank You, heavenly Father. Amen.

(*Little Folded Hands*, p. 5)

Almighty and everlasting God,
Thank You that You have brought me safely
to the beginning of another day.

Keep me from sinful thoughts and actions and from
running into dangerous situations.

Help me in everything I do, and guide me always to
do only what is good in Your sight. Amen.

(Adapted from a morning collect)

Thank You, God,
    For making the world and all that is in it,
    For making my body and mind,
    For my home, my parents, and all the people who
    love and care for me,

For food to eat and clothes to wear,

For leading me to know Jesus, my Savior,

For Baptism and the gifts of the Holy Spirit.

Thank You, God, for everything. Amen.

God the Father,

Please keep us in Your care;

Lord Jesus, be our constant friend;

Holy Spirit, guide us in all we do.

Bless us and protect us until we come to the end of our journey. Amen.

(Adapted from a traveler's blessing)

Have mercy on me, O God, according to Your steadfast love; according to Your abundant mercy blot out my transgressions. Wash me thoroughly from my iniquity, and cleanse me from my sin! . . . Create in me a clean heart, O God, and renew a right spirit within me.

(Psalm 51:1–2, 10)

May the peace of God, which passes all understanding, keep our hearts and minds in the knowledge and love of God, and of His Son, Jesus Christ our Lord; and the blessing of God almighty, the Father, the Son, and the Holy Spirit, be with us and remain with us always. Amen.

(Traditional)

Daily Prayers

Sunday

Heavenly Father, it's Sunday! On this day, we join with other believers to worship You. We ask that Your Holy Spirit prepare our hearts to receive the Gospel message that we'll hear in church. Bless Your Word and all those who hear it today. Strengthen our faith so that we may trust in the grace and mercy You provide to us through Jesus Christ, our Redeemer. Forgive our sins—all those things we say and do and think that offend You. May we carry the joy of worship with us until the next time we join others to praise and worship You. May we be faithful witnesses to You in all we say and do today and in the week ahead. In Jesus' name we pray. Amen.

Monday

Dear Lord, sometimes the weekends seem so short and we're not happy when Monday comes again. But today, Lord, we thank You for weekend downtime when we can rest or enjoy activities or spend time with family and friends. We thank You for the opportunity we had to worship You yesterday. We're sorry for the wrong things we've done already today, and we ask, Lord, that You forgive us. Thank You for another Monday, when our week begins anew. May our actions and words give honor to You, Lord. Bless us now as we set out to work and to school, and keep us faithful to serve You and others. We pray in Jesus' name. Amen.

Lord Jesus Christ, thank You for the food we had at breakfast and for the home we leave as we go about our day. There are so many people who don't have these things—people who don't have enough food to eat or clothes to wear; people who don't have homes to call their own. We ask You, Jesus, to look after those who are less fortunate than we are. We ask You to provide for them by whatever means are available. If there is someone we can help, show us opportunity to help. We ask You, Lord, to take care of everyone who serves the needy in Your name. Bless them and keep them faithful to serve You as they serve others. Amen.

Wednesday

Heavenly Father, today we thank You for people who have positions of leadership and authority. We thank You for bosses and teachers, for government officials and lawmakers. We understand that You created order to the world so that there would be peace and safety for all people. Protect and guide those who are in charge of earthly things, Lord, so that we may enjoy a safe world and go about our day. When we make mistakes or when bad things happen, we ask that You forgive our sins and preserve us from harm and danger. In all things, Lord, may we give all glory to You. In Jesus' name we pray. Amen.

Thursday

Lord and Creator, we know that You have a plan for us. You have created us with abilities and gifts that will work toward fulfilling Your plan. Ultimately, You plan for us to live with You in heaven. Until then, we ask that You bless us in our work, whether that is at school or on the job. We ask that You send Your Spirit to keep us faithful to You in all we do and say. Help us to honor You with our actions and behavior toward others. In Jesus' name and for His sake we pray. Amen.

Father God, there are many temptations in the world; there are many problems and bad things. We ask that You send Your Holy Spirit to keep us faithful to You so that we might never forget Your blessings. As our week draws to an end, we ask that the Holy Spirit guide our thoughts and deeds so that all we do and say honors You. May our weekend rest, relaxation, and activities help to restore our bodies and minds so that we are ever mindful of Your mercy. In Jesus' name we pray. Amen.

Saturday

Dear God, whether it's a busy Saturday or a relaxing one, we thank You and praise You that we have this day to enjoy one another. We thank You for Your protection and faithfulness, that we can always be certain of Your grace and mercy through Jesus Christ. We ask Your continued protection that we may be safe from harm and danger, that we may be preserved from Satan's wicked ways, and that we may be healed in body and spirit. Lord, always keep us mindful of Your promises of forgiveness and salvation. Through Jesus and in Jesus we pray. Amen.

Special Days

New Year's Day—Almighty God, Your mercies are new every morning. We praise You that You have brought us to this new day in a new year. Grant that, in the coming year, we may honor You and live as faithful witnesses to Your love for us through Jesus Christ. We pray in His name and for His sake. Amen.

Valentine's Day—God of love, thank You for loving us! Help us to love others. In the name of Jesus Christ, who is love. Amen.

Presidents' Day—Almighty God, today we honor those who have served our country as president. We thank You that You have blessed us with faithful leaders who have loved You and who have served our nation with integrity and honor. May we follow their example of faithful leadership, wisdom, and service to others. Please bless us with presidents who find joy in their work and who confess Your Word and uphold it. In the name of Christ Jesus we pray. Amen.

Palm Sunday—We praise You and glorify You, Lord Jesus! We raise our hosannas so that everyone may know that You are our Lord and King! Be with us today and every day, that we may abide in Your grace and mercy. Amen.

Maundy Thursday—Lord Jesus Christ, today is the day we remember the Holy Supper You instituted for our benefit. For those of us who have received instruction in this sacred gift, we ask that we might receive it in faith and for our benefit. Oh, refresh us! For those of us who are not receiving Holy Communion, we ask Your blessing, that we may stay firm in our faith and remember our Baptism; for You live and reign with the Father and the Holy Spirit, one God, now and forever. Amen.

Good Friday—Dear Jesus, our Savior and Redeemer, today we observe the terrible day on which You willingly went to the cross to suffer and die for us. Such love is beyond our comprehension. However, we also know that this is a glorious day: as we focus on Your cross, we are reminded that through Your death You paid the ultimate price for our sins. You brought us out of darkness and made us right with God. You won final victory over eternal death so that we might have eternal life with You and the Father and the Holy Spirit. Amen.

Easter—Lord Jesus, today we are dressed in our best clothes and we are going to church to celebrate Your victory over sin, death, and the devil. The Bible tells us that You rose from the grave on the first Easter morning so that we can know the promise of eternal life with You. Thank You, Jesus! Praise You, Jesus! Thank You, Jesus! Amen.

Mother's Day—Lord God, thank You for our mom and for all the things she does for us. Thank You for choosing her to be our mom and for choosing us to be her kids. We're especially glad that she is faithful to You and teaches us about You! Help us always to honor and love her, to obey her and respect her. In Jesus' name we pray. Amen.

Father's Day—Heavenly Father, today we thank You for our dad and for all the things he does for us. Thank You for choosing him to be our dad and for choosing us to be his kids. We're especially glad that he is faithful to You and teaches us about You! Help us always to honor and love him, to obey him and respect him. In Jesus' name we pray. Amen.

Independence Day—Lord of the nations, although we celebrate this day with parades and fireworks and fun, we take a minute now to remember that our nation was founded under Your name. You have preserved and sustained our country in times of trouble and of peace. Let us not take our freedom for granted; rather, let us remember that true freedom comes from serving You and others in Your name. Grant us wisdom to choose faithful leadership at all levels of government and to honor, respect, and obey those in positions of authority. Guide them and keep them as they serve us. Accept our praise and thanks for our nation and our freedoms. In the name of Jesus, who freed us from slavery to sin and eternal damnation, we pray. Amen.

Halloween—Dear Jesus, today we have fun with costumes and candy, with pumpkins and spooky stories. We ask that You protect us from the evil things in the world, that You guard us against harm and danger, and that You send Your Holy Spirit to keep us firm in our faith in You as our Savior and Lord. Amen.

Thanksgiving—Dear God, we praise You and bless You for giving us all good things. Today we celebrate the gifts and blessings of our land, and we thank You for the gifts of food and family, for our nation and the freedom to worship You. Grant that we may always enjoy these privileges. Keep us firm in the one true faith that Your Word is pure and that Jesus is our Savior. In His holy name we pray. Amen.

Christmas Eve—Lord God, heavenly Father, tonight we celebrate that holy night on which You sent Jesus to be our Savior. Let us keep our focus on the baby in the manger and not on the things that distract us from Him. Let us always remember that the very best gift is Jesus, our Savior, who came so that we might have forgiveness of sins and the promise of salvation through Him and in Him. Amen.

Christmas Day—Dearest Jesus, holy Child, hear us as we pray. Lead us and guide us with joy on this day. Keep us and save us and help us obey. We praise You and thank You that You love us always. Amen.

New Year's Eve—Lord God, heavenly Father, tonight, as the year draws to a close, we turn our thoughts and hearts to the blessings of the last twelve months and to Your many good gifts to us. We thank You that You have brought us to this night and that You have kept us in faith in You. We praise You that You have delivered us from hardship and bad days and that You give us the hope of a bright tomorrow. We pray in the name of Jesus Christ, our Lord, who lives and reigns with You and the Holy Spirit. Amen.

First Day of Autumn—Heavenly Father, You made the world and everything in it. You designed the years to pass and the seasons to come. On this first day of autumn, we thank You for Your beautiful creation and for providing for us through it. In Jesus' name we pray. Amen.

First Day of Winter—Dear God, as the season changes from autumn to winter, we are reminded of what comes next: Christmas! Thank You, God, for sending Jesus to be our Savior from sin. In His name we pray. Amen.

First Day of Spring—Lord Jesus, as spring begins today, we are reminded of the life and hope You provide. We know that we have these blessings only because You give them. We have life because God created us and because You come to us in the words of the Bible and in the sacraments we receive at church. We have hope because You came to forgive the sins of the world and to offer salvation and eternal life. Thank You, Jesus! Amen.

First Day of Summer—Lord God, thank You for summer. Thank You for long, warm days and for special time with family and friends. We ask, Lord, that You draw us closer to You, that You show us Your ways, and that You guide us through Your Word and through Your servants. May all we do give You glory and honor this season and throughout the year. We ask this for Jesus' sake. Amen.

SCHOOL

First Day—Dear Jesus, it's the first day of a new school year. I am excited and a little worried. I ask that You guide me and bless me on this day and in the year ahead. Bless the teachers and the other students in my class. Bless all the other workers at my school, those who work in the cafeteria and office, those who drive buses, and those who work to keep the school clean and safe. May I honor You in my thoughts, words, and actions. May I reflect Your love for others and show mercy in Your name. Amen.

Last Day—Dear God, it's the last day of school for this year, and I want to celebrate! It's a relief to get to this day, but it's also a little sad. Today I'll say good-bye to some people and "see you later" to others. The whole summer is ahead, but for today, I'm looking back at the school year I just finished. Thank You, God, for the year of learning and growing. Thank You for all the fun I had with my friends. Thank You for the opportunities I had to discover and explore new things. In Jesus' name I pray. Amen.

For Teachers, Staff, and School—Dear Lord God, it's by Your mercy and provision that we can come to You with prayers about teachers, school staff, and all the students at ____ school. We ask that You make ____ a good place to learn and a safe place to be. Bless all the teachers and staff at the school. Bless all the students there too. May we all have the desire to learn and grow as You would have us. May we all resist temptation to do wrong things. May we all give You glory in what we say and do. Please send Your Holy Spirit to keep us faithful to You throughout all our days. In Jesus' name we pray. Amen.

Before a Test (Confident)—Heavenly Father, I've learned a lot and studied hard. I'm ready. When I take my test today, I ask that You help me concentrate and remember all that I've learned so I can do well. Help me always to remember that I can do all things through Jesus, who strengthens me. In His name I pray. Amen.

Before a Test (Nervous)—Lord God, I've tried very hard to learn and I have tried to understand the lessons. I'm still nervous about it, however. I'm not sure

I'm ready to take this test today. When test time comes, help me to stay calm and rely on You for courage and strength. Even if I don't do well, please help me to remember that because of Jesus, You love me no matter what. There's nothing on this earth that can separate me from Him. I pray in Jesus' name and for His sake. Amen.

Report Cards (Confident)—Dear Lord God, it's report card day, and I'm excited. I think I got good grades. Please help me to remember that You gave me everything I have and everything I need. You gave me my abilities and my intellect, my eyes, ears, and all my senses. May I always give You honor and glory in everything I do and say and think. Thank You, God. In Jesus' name I pray. Amen.

Report Cards (Nervous)—Heavenly Father, it's report card day, and I'm nervous. I'm not sure that I did all that well. In fact, I think I might have some bad grades. Please help me to try to do better next time. Help me always to remember that my real value comes because of what Jesus has done for me. I am forgiven because of Jesus. I am saved because of Jesus. I will have eternal life because of Jesus. In His name I pray. Amen.

Before School Care—Dear God, our day starts early, even before school starts. Keep us safe as we begin our day. Bless us in all we do and say. Bless those who work at day care. Keep us all in Your loving mercy. In Jesus' name we pray. Amen.

After School Care—Dear Lord, thank You for the people who take care of us after school. Now that we have ended our day, we ask that You bless our journey home and our evening together. Keep us safe as we drive. Please send Your Holy Spirit, that we may be ever faithful to You. In Jesus' name we pray. Amen.

Do I Have to Go to School Today?—Lord God, heavenly Father, I don't want to go to school today. I would rather stay home and play or go somewhere else, anywhere else but school. I know that isn't an option. I know that I have to go to school—but I still don't want to. So, God, I'm asking You to change my heart so I will appreciate school. Help me to like learning. Help me to understand that going to school is the special job You have in mind for me right now. Please bless me at school today, Lord. I really need it. I ask this in Jesus' name. Amen.

Homework—Dear Jesus, it's the end of the day and we're ready to go home, and that means it's homework time. I know that I have to focus. Help me to resist distractions so I can do the best job that I'm able to do. Help me to learn with pleasure so I can honor my teacher and respect [his or her] efforts. Help me to honor You and serve You in all that I do. Amen.

Trouble with the Teacher—Heavenly Father, I'm pretty sure my teacher doesn't like me. Well, at least I think so. [He or she] always seems mad and sometimes says things that make me feel bad. Help me to remember that being a teacher isn't always easy. Help me to do my best at school and to behave the right way. Please help me to remember that You love everyone, even when I'm not feeling friendly toward [him or her]. In Jesus' name I pray. Amen.

Field Trip—It's a special day, dear Jesus, and we are all excited about it. ____'s class is taking a break from the everyday school routine to go to ____. The opportunity to see and do something new is especially fun. Help____to keep eyes and ears open so [he or she] learns new things today. Help ____ to use [his or her] learning and new experience for good. Help [him or her] to pay attention to the teacher and chaperones and behave in a way that honors You and pleases them. We ask that You keep safe____ and all others who take this field trip today. Please protect them from all harm and danger. Thank You, Jesus! Amen.

Feelings, Situations, and Others

Game Day—Heavenly Father, as we leave home for a _____ game, we ask that You help _____ use the gifts, talents, and abilities that You've given to glorify You and represent You. Help ____ to do [his or her] best and to show good sportsmanship, no matter how the game turns out. Win or lose, we belong to You. Thank You, Lord God, for the most important victory of all—Jesus' victory over sin, death, and the devil. In His name and for His sake we pray. Amen.

We Won the Game—Lord God, by Your mercy and grace, we were able to play well today and win our game. Thank You! We praise You for good health, strong bodies, our team, and our coach. Protect us from the sin of pride and boastfulness, that we may honor You with our actions and give You glory for all good things. We ask this in Jesus' name. Amen.

We Lost the Game—Dear Jesus, everybody wants to win. Nobody wants to lose. It's easy to be a bad sport about losing. It's tempting to say mean things about the other team or to complain or even to cry. Forgive us if we do that. Forgive us for feeling bad about not winning. Help us to remember that although we didn't win our game, we aren't losers. That's because You won victory over the worst opponent: Satan. Your death on the cross might have seemed like losing to some people, but we know that Your victory over sin, death, and the evil one means that we are winners too. Jesus, help us to remember that Yours is the only victory that really counts. Amen.

Feeling Sick—Dear Jesus, I'm feeling sick but not sick enough to stay home. I know that people call You the Great Physician. Please help me feel better. Please also heal me of all my sins. Thank You, Jesus. Amen.

Injury—Dear God, You know that I have an injury. In fact, You know everything. Please heal my injury so I can be back to normal. As I'm healing, help me to remember that You made the world and everything in it. You made me and all the people I know. Keep us safe and help us grow in body and in faith in You. I pray this in Jesus' name. Amen.

About Something Sad—Heavenly Father, I'm sad today. There's something heavy on my heart and I want to cry. I know that the Bible is full of stories about sad things, and I know that no matter what happens, You have plans for those who believe in You. Your plan is perfect and beautiful and happy. Your plan means that You sent Jesus to save me from all sadness and sin and bad things. Sad things will still happen here, but because of Jesus, one day, when I'm in heaven with You, I will never be sad again. Thank You, God, for having things under control. Thank You for loving me for Jesus' sake. Amen.

About Something Good or Happy—Dear Lord God, since You understand everything about us, then You know how happy we are because of _____. Thank You, Lord, for the good things that we have and that happen in our lives. We praise You, Lord, because we know that all good things come from You. Fill our hearts with joy, Lord, and keep us mindful of the blessings You provide. We praise You, Lord, because You love us! We praise You, Lord, for the best gift ever— Jesus. In His name we pray. Amen.

Trouble with Friends—Dear Jesus, I'm not getting along with _____. That feels pretty bad. I feel sad and hurt and angry, and I wish _____ and I were friends. I know that some people didn't like You. I know that they hurt You very badly and they sent You to the cross to die. That terrible thing ended up being a good thing because that's how You earned forgiveness for the whole world. Forgive me, Lord. Forgive _____ too. I hope _____ and I can be friends, but if not, then help me to remember that You are my best friend no matter what. Amen.

There's Someone I Don't Like—Lord Jesus, there's someone I don't like and it's hard to pray for [him or her]. However, I know that You command us to love our enemies. I ask that You help me remember that You love everyone and that everyone has a special place in the world. We're all different because God the Father designed us that way. Help me overcome my bad feelings and show respect and compassion to everyone. Open my heart so I can see the good in everyone. Lord Jesus, I ask for Your forgiveness and mercy. Amen.

Friends—Lord Jesus, You are our very best friend. Thank You! We have other friends too, and we thank You for them too! Today we ask that You bless our friends and guide them with Your Word by Your Holy Spirit. Help us to be kind to one another and sensitive to one another's needs and feelings. We ask that we may be a blessing to our friends and share Your joy with them so that they may be certain of Your promise of forgiveness and salvation. Amen.

Family—Lord God, heavenly Father, You designed families at the creation of the world. You gave us one another so we can have joy and love, protection and security. Thank You for the blessings of our family! Today we ask that You keep our family from harm and danger and that You protect us from sin and evil. Forgive us for the times we have let someone down, offended a loved one, or acted out in anger. Grant that we may always know You and trust in Your faithfulness, that we may have life everlasting through Your Son, Jesus Christ. Amen.

Neighbors—Lord Jesus, You taught us what being a good neighbor really means: helping those who are in need, regardless of who they are. Today we ask that You show us our neighbors and guide us in ways we can be helpful to them. If those near us are in need, make us mindful of ways we can help. If they know You, let us rejoice with them. If they have not come to faith in You, grant that we may seek opportunity to share Your Gospel so that they may receive salvation through You. Amen.

Getting Along with Siblings—Dear God, some of the stories You put in the Bible are about siblings who didn't get along. Some of the siblings were really mean to one another. I understand about not getting along. My [brother or sister] is really bugging me, and I don't like it. Getting along is hard. Sometimes I don't want to get along. However, I know this attitude is wrong, and I am sorry about it. Please forgive me, God, for the bad things I say and do and for not wanting to get along. Please forgive my [brother or sister] too. Help us to do better next time and to show that we love one another. Help us to remember that we can love one another because Jesus loved us first. In His name and for His sake we pray. Amen.

For Bad News in Our Community—Lord of peace, God of grace, our hearts are heavy at today's news. People are suffering. Please help them. Don't let them despair. Send Your Holy Spirit, that they may know Your love and mercy. Let us see how we may be a help to them, and bless those who are on hand to offer their care and services. Keep us steadfast in faith so that we, too, may know Your love and mercy and know the peace of our Lord Jesus Christ, who lives and reigns with You and the Holy Spirit, now and forever. Amen.

Starting the Morning on the Wrong Foot—It seems that everything is going wrong today, Lord. I wish I could just start the whole day over. But it's time to go, and even though I feel like I'm not ready for this day to start, I know that I don't have a real choice. So, Lord, I ask that You forgive me for my negative thoughts. I ask that You help me to repent of my sins. I ask that You send Your Holy Spirit so that I may rejoice in today—because You made this day. In Jesus' name I pray. Amen.

Feeling Crabby—Dear God, some days are just not happy. Some days I just want to be crabby. I know that this is wrong, though. I know that being crabby makes things difficult for others and makes my own bad mood even worse. I ask that You help me remember all the good things in my life—a loving family, a good home, friends, a beautiful world, and Jesus. Help me turn my thoughts to my Savior so I can remember that He takes away my sins—all of them, even the sin of just being crabby. Forgive me for my bad mood. Thank You for loving me even when I don't deserve it. I pray in Jesus' name. Amen.

A Fight First Thing in the Morning—Dear Savior, it's been a difficult day already, and there is much to pray about. Sometimes we hurt people because we're angry or selfish or not feeling well. Sometimes we hurt others because they hurt us first. We're truly sorry about all of it. We need Your forgiveness. We're thankful that You never get tired of forgiving us. Have mercy on us, Lord, and send Your Holy Spirit so that we may show one another kindness, mercy, love, and forgiveness. Amen.

Disobedience—Jesus Christ, our Redeemer and Savior, You know how hard it is to obey. You know because You came to save the world from disobedience. Your suffering and death on the cross were the obedient and loving acts of a loving Lord—all because You love us even when we disobey. We do not want to sin; we want to be good. We're sorry. We ask that You forgive us for our disobedience. Please take away our bad thoughts, words, and actions, and help us to treat others as You treat us. Amen.

Forgiving Others—Lord Jesus, it's hard to forgive others. It's especially hard when they've done something wrong and I haven't. However, I know that You forgive us for our sins. I know that You forgive ___, and because of that, I can forgive [him or her] too. Protect me against the sins of anger, selfishness, pride, and stubbornness. Open my heart so I may enjoy the blessings of forgiveness, which You offer through Your suffering and death on the cross. Thank You, Lord. Amen.

Rejoicing—Gracious God, this is the day You have made. Let us rejoice and be glad in it! We thank You for Your wonderful creation, for making us just how we are, and for continuing to care for us and provide for us. All these good things come to us because You love us, and not because we have done anything to earn them. Help us to live in such a way that others may know You and Your good gifts. Thank You especially for Jesus, our Savior and Redeemer. To Him be the glory! Amen.

Good Health—Heavenly Father, today we thank You for good health and we praise Your name. In Your mercy, may we continue to enjoy strong bodies and live joyfully through the days You have given us. May we never take for granted the gift of good health. Guard us and guide us so that we may remain faithful to You and live our lives in Your grace and power. We pray in the name of Christ Jesus. Amen.

Peace in the World—Merciful God, the world is filled turmoil and hatred and evil. Sometimes it seems as if people will never get along and that Satan will win. But we know that You are the Lord of all; You are bigger and stronger and more powerful than any evil. You are the Lord of peace. Help us remember that Jesus defeated Satan and all sin when He died on the cross. Keep our hearts and minds focused on His victory and the peace that only He can give. In His holy name we pray. Amen.

For Our Country—Almighty God, Lord of the universe, we praise You and thank You for our nation. Bless our government leaders and workers, that they might serve with wisdom, integrity, and honor. Bless our military personnel, that they might protect us from harm and defend us in times of trouble. Bless our land with prosperity, that we may have enough to share with those who are in need. Give us thankful hearts, that we might not take for granted our nation and our freedom, especially the freedom to worship You. Please grant that in all things we trust in You that Your will be done. Amen.

For Our Sunday School—Heavenly Father, grant us the desire to learn more about You and Your Holy Word. Bless our teachers, that they may joyfully instruct us in the true faith. Open our minds that we may have greater understanding of the benefits of Sunday School, and open our hearts that we may have stronger faith, greater hope, and deeper love for You. Grant that we may truly enjoy the great gifts You give to us in Christ Jesus. Amen.

For Vacation Bible School—Lord God, we are so excited finally to be on the way to VBS. We'll see our friends, play games, have snacks, sing songs, and make great crafts. We can't wait. We know the most important thing about VBS is learning about our God and about Jesus, our Savior, from the Bible. Thank You for faith to believe Your Word. Thank You for the fun of Vacation Bible School! In Jesus' name we pray. Amen.

After Vacation Bible School—Dear Jesus, please bless us through what we learned about You in VBS. You are our Savior, who died and rose again. You give us forgiveness for our sins and life forever with You in heaven. That's great news to hear from the Bible! Help us pass on the message of VBS to our friends and family. In Your name we pray. Amen.

School Play or Concert—Lord God, You bless us with the gifts of creativity, music, and drama. Help us use these gifts to Your glory so that others will come to stronger faith in You and Your Son, Jesus Christ, and have a greater understanding of Your Word and its benefit to us. May our play or concert be a testimony to You and Your great love for us, that we may share in Your divine gifts and receive the fullness of eternal life with You. In Jesus' name we pray. Amen.

Graduation—What a blessing, Lord, to be graduating. By Your will, I have accomplished a goal—a big one! Now it's the end of one phase of my life and the beginning of another. I know that You love me. Although I have plans for what I want to do in my life, I know that only You know my future. I trust that You will lead me and guide me in Your ways, that I might serve You and others in Jesus' name. May I always have Your Word to light my path. May my life be a blessing to others and a faithful witness to Your goodness through Christ Jesus. Amen.

Answered Prayer—Gracious God, we praise You and thank You for answered prayer. We know that You hear all prayers in Jesus' name. We know that You work all things for the good of those who love You. We do love You, Lord. We thank You that You have generously given us what we asked. In the name of Jesus Christ, our Savior and Redeemer, we pray. Amen.

Unanswered Prayer—Heavenly Father, we've been praying for ___ and that hasn't happened. Send Your Holy Spirit to strengthen our faith so that we rely on You and trust that You are in control. Help us to pray as Jesus did: not our will, but Yours, be done. In His holy name we pray. Amen.

Being Frightened—Dear Jesus, I'm afraid. Help me trust You. Help me to know that You love me and will never leave me. Help me to remember that You will protect me from danger and defend me from evil. Help me to know that even when bad things happen, You will always love me and will always be with me. Amen.

Someone Made Fun of Me—Dear Jesus, You are my best friend. You love me and I love You. Today something happened that made me feel really bad. _____ made fun of me. Other kids laughed. I was embarrassed and I just wanted to run away. Please help me remember that bad things happen because there is sin in the world. Help me to remember that You forgive _____, even though [he or she] did something wrong. Help me to forgive [him or her] too. That is hard to do. But I will try to forgive because I know that You have forgiven me when I do wrong things. Thank You, Jesus. Amen.

I Hurt Someone's Feelings—Lord God, You know everything about me, and You know what I did today. I hurt _____'s feelings. I'm very sorry. I shouldn't have said or done that. It was mean, and I feel bad that I hurt [his or her] feelings. Please forgive me, God. Please help me to have courage to ask _____ for forgiveness and to say I'm sorry. Help [him or her] to forgive me for what I said or did. Please help me to remember to show Jesus' love to other people. In His name I pray. Amen.

Someone Bullied Me—Dear Jesus, You know better than anyone what it feels like to have someone be mean to You. It's a terrible feeling. I want _____ to stop being mean to me. I ask that You help [him or her] see that it's wrong to be a bully and that [he or she] should be nice instead. Help [him or her] to know You and to want to please You. Also, and this is the hardest part, I ask that You forgive [him or her] of [his or her] sins. Help me forgive [him or her] too. Please forgive me for my mean thoughts and anger. Amen.

I Was a Bully—Dear Jesus, today I was a bully. I'm so sorry. I don't know why I did it. I will try not to do it again. I know that You love everyone and that You forgive all our sins. Please forgive me. Please help ___ to forgive me for being mean. Please help me learn to make good choices, to be nice to others even if they're not nice to me, and to resist temptation when others are misbehaving. Amen.

We're on the Go!

Long Drive Ahead—Lord God, our Creator and Protector, You made the earth and everything in it. The Bible tells us that You watch over the little sparrow and provide for all creatures. We ask that You protect and keep us as we travel. Watch over us so that no evil comes to us. Bring us safely to the end of our journey. Please keep us faithful to You and mindful of Your gifts to us. In Jesus' name we pray. Amen.

Vacation—Dear heavenly Father, we thank You for all Your good gifts to us. Today we thank You especially for the gift of time off from work and school. Although we're taking a break from our regular schedule and responsibilities, we ask that You keep us faithful so that we never take a break from loving and serving You. Bless us and protect us as we enjoy this special time together. Keep us from all harm and danger, and grant that we use our vacation time to refresh our minds and bodies so we may better serve You in all we do. In Jesus' name we pray. Amen.

Safely Home Again—Dear Lord God, thank You for Your protection as we traveled away from home and back again. Thank You for delivering us from harm and for keeping us safe in our activities. Now that we've returned, we ask that You bless our home and our family and keep us ever faithful to You. Send Your Holy Spirit so that we might repent of our sins and live in righteousness through Jesus Christ. Amen.

Bad Weather—Dear Lord God, we know You are the Creator of all things and that You have power over all things. Today, as we leave the safety of our home, we face challenging driving conditions. We ask that You send Your heavenly angels so that no harm might come to us as we travel. If it is Your will, may we safely reach our destination. Lord, protect us and defend us. Strengthen our faith and guard us against evil. Keep our hearts and minds in Christ Jesus. In His holy name we pray. Amen.

Rainy Day—Lord Jesus, Son of God, we know that You have power over the wind and rain. When Your disciples cried out to You in fear, you calmed the storm and protected them. We ask that You protect us, too, as we go out in the rain today. Keep us safe as we drive on wet roads, and guard those who have to work outside in the rain. Help us remember that rain is a wonderful gift that helps all living things. Please help us remember that it is water and Your Word that made us Your precious children in Baptism. Amen.

Sunny Day—What a beautiful sunny day, Lord! Thank You for creating it! Thank You for bringing us safely through the night to this day. As we go about our day, we ask that You send Your Holy Spirit to keep us mindful of all the beauty in the world around us. Help us to be good stewards of the world You created. Help us to stay faithful to You, and keep us from falling into sin. We pray for Your protection for us and for those we love. Bless our family and our friends. In Jesus' name we pray. Amen.

Dinner Out—Dear Jesus, it's a blessing to be able to go out to dinner together. We're thankful that we have the opportunity to enjoy times such as this. Keep us mindful, Lord, about those who aren't so blessed. We're thankful for the food we will eat as we share this special time together. Most importantly, we're thankful for You, Jesus, and for Your great gifts of forgiveness, peace, and promised salvation that You provide in Your Holy Meal. Amen.

Home from Dinner Out—Lord God, provider of all good things, thank You for the gift of food for the nourishment of our bodies and the benefit of our minds. May we be blessed by Your provision, through Jesus Christ, Your dear Son, who lives and reigns with You forever. Amen.

Road Construction—Heavenly Father, it's easy to see road construction as a nuisance: it causes inconvenient delays in our travel. Help us to remember that construction is a good thing: it means better roads and bridges so we can be safe as we drive. It also provides jobs for people who have special skills, equipment, and materials. We ask that You keep the other travelers and the workers safe. We thank You, God, for road construction. In Jesus' name we pray. Amen.

Sleepover—Dear God, we're having a sleepover tonight, and we're all excited. It's so good to have friends and to have the opportunity to enjoy fun times together. Help us to remember You, Lord, so that we honor You and give You glory with our thoughts and words and actions. Guard us against the temptation to make bad choices. Most of all, we thank You for the gift of Your Son, Jesus, who loves us, forgives us, and brings us the hope of eternal life with You. In His name we pray. Amen.

Doctor or Dentist Visit (Healthy)—Dear God, today _____ has a checkup at the _____ . Although checkups sometimes make us all a little nervous, we know that this is a time to celebrate the body You have given [him or her]. We praise You and thank You for Your wonderful creation. We praise You and thank You for the gift of good health. Grant continued good health for _____, and be with the doctor and other medical staff we'll see today. Help us to take good care of our bodies so we can be examples of Your love and of the life that You give. We pray this in Jesus' name. Amen.

Doctor or Dentist Visit (Sick)—Lord Jesus, it's when we are not well that we appreciate good health the most. When You walked among people on earth, You showed compassion as You brought forgiveness and healing to people. We come to You today to ask that You grant forgiveness and healing to ___, if it is Your will. People call You the Great Physician because You have the power to heal all sickness of both the body and the spirit. Thank You for healing _____ of the sickness of sin. We ask that You heal [his or her] sickness of body too. Amen.

Going to a Wedding—Father in heaven, You created man and woman to be together and praise You with their lives. We ask that You bless _____ and _____ on their wedding day today, that they may enjoy a long and joyful marriage, and that they remain faithful to You and to each other. May they follow the perfect example of marriage that Jesus gives as the Bridegroom of the Church. Bless all married people, Lord, that they love one another and that they honor You with their lives. In Jesus' name we pray. Amen.

Going to Visit a New Baby—Abba, Father, we praise You and thank You for this new life, which You have created. We're excited to meet _____ . We praise You and give thanks to You for this wonderful gift of life. In Your mercy, Lord, grant _____ good health and growth. Be with [his or her] parents, and keep them faithful to You as they bring up this baby in a loving home. We pray that they bring _____ to the font, where [he or she] will receive the blessings of Baptism. We ask these things in Jesus' name. Amen.

Going to a Funeral or Visitation—You number our days, O Lord, and You alone know how long our lives will be. May we live as faithful witnesses to Your mercy and grace until our last day on earth. Today, we are going to pay our respects to the family of _____. May we be a blessing to them as they mourn the loss of their loved one. Grant them peace and assurances of salvation through Christ Jesus. In His name and for His sake we pray. Amen.

Going to Visit Someone in the Hospital—Jesus, You are our Great Physician. You can heal all illness. If it's Your will, Lord, we ask that You heal _____ and restore [him or her] to health. Going to a hospital makes us a little uncomfortable, but we ask that our visit would be a blessing and a pleasure to _____ and that we might bring joy and hope to [him or her]. In Your mercy, we ask that You guide the hospital staff and medical professionals as they care for _____. Amen.

Going to an Amusement Park or Carnival—It's a special day for us, Lord, and we know that all good things are gifts from You because You love us. Guard our hearts and minds, that we might bring You glory in all we say and do. Send Your holy angels to protect us from harm and danger. Thank You, Lord, that we can spend this day having fun together. In Jesus' name we pray. Amen.

Going to the Library—Heavenly Father, as we set out today to go to the library, we remember to thank You for the gifts of books and technology. Reading teaches us about the great world we live in—the world You made! May our selections at the library be good for our minds and be pleasing to You. In Jesus' name we pray. Amen.

Going out for Ice Cream—Dear God, it's so much fun to go out for ice cream. It's a special treat, and we are thankful. Thank You for special treats and for the occasion to enjoy them. May we always remember that all good things come from You because You love us. The very best thing You sent us was Jesus, our Redeemer and Savior. In His name we pray. Amen.

Going to a Movie—Gracious Lord, we give You thanks for the goodness of Your creation and for leisure time to spend as we see fit. We know that there are many things in this world that seek to distract us from You and from the gifts You generously give. Guard us against the temptation to be led astray by the ways of the world. Protect us from wickedness and evil that might harm us. Send Your Holy Spirit, that we might stay strong in our faith and seek You first. We pray in Jesus' name. Amen.

Going to a Volunteer or Service Project—Lord Jesus, it's a pleasure and a joy to serve people in Your name. Grant that we may be a help to others who can benefit from the things we can do. May we serve them with humility and love, with joy and kindness, so they can know You and Your mercy through us. To that end, grant that we may be faithful witnesses to the work that You do for us—forgiveness of sin and life everlasting. Amen.

Going to the Grocery Store—It's a chore, Lord, but it's a blessing too. Going to the grocery store is part of our family's routine, and sometimes there are things we'd rather be doing instead. But food is necessary for our bodies, and the grocery store is a blessing that we sometimes take for granted—especially when we don't want to be there. Forgive our selfishness, Lord. Keep us mindful of those who don't have enough food. Thank You for Your provision. Thank You especially for providing us with the Bread of Life, who sustains us unto eternity. We pray in Jesus' name. Amen.

Going Shopping—What a blessing, Lord, to be able to go shopping today. We are grateful for Your provision, which allows us to buy what we need. Help us put all things in proper perspective so that we resist the temptation to spend money aimlessly and from wanting more than we need. Keep us safe from harm and protect us from evil as we venture out today. In Jesus' name we pray. Amen.

Having the Car Serviced—Dear God, today we have to get our car serviced. Be with us as we travel and keep us from danger along the way. Remind us that a car is a great responsibility and a gift from Your generous hand. Thank You for people who choose car repair as a job. Bless them in their work. In Jesus' name we pray. Amen.

Car Trouble at Home—Dear Lord, the bad news is that the car broke down even before we left home. The good news is that we're still safe at home. Car trouble is such a nuisance, and it's easy to lose our temper or be upset. Guide us from sinful anger, Lord, and lead us to patience and self-control. If it is Your will, Lord, may we be able to get the car fixed quickly and at little expense. If getting our car fixed isn't so easy or quick, then we ask that You allow us to remember that You turn all things to good for those that love You. We do love You, Lord! In Jesus' name we pray. Amen.

Car Trouble on the Road—Dear Jesus, we are having car trouble along the side of the road. It's frightening and upsetting to have trouble when we're away from home. We ask that You keep us safe from harm as we wait for someone to come help us. We ask that You calm our fears and ease our worries as we wait. In a little boat on a stormy sea, You calmed the disciples' fears and reminded them to trust in You above all things. Keep us focused on You, Lord, so that no matter what happens, we will trust in Your mercy, protection, forgiveness, and salvation. Amen.

Getting Lost—Almighty God, we're lost and a little frightened. You are our refuge, Lord, and our stronghold in times of trouble. Right now, when we don't know where we are, we ask that You keep us safe from harm and deliver us from evil. Grant us patience as we endure this moment of confusion, and keep us firm in our faith, that we might trust in Your protection and provision. We pray in Jesus' name. Amen.

Driving in the Dark—Lord Jesus, You are our Good Shepherd. Just as the shepherd calls the sheep to himself for protection and safety, You call us to You for protection from evil and for safety from the harmful things in our world. Now, as we make our way in the darkness of night, we ask that You grant us continued protection against all harm. Send Your holy angels to be with us and guard us. Please grant us safe travels until we reach our destination. Amen.

Fire Truck, Ambulance, or Police—Gracious God, the sirens are blaring, and that means someone is in trouble. We ask You to be with those in distress, that they may receive help quickly and, if it is Your will, that they may be healed of their illness or injury. Be with the emergency workers too. Guide them and guard them so that no harm comes to them. Grant them wisdom and skill in their work. Please keep all those around them out of harm's way. We pray in the name of Christ Jesus. Amen.

Getting a Cast Taken Off—Thank You, Lord, for healing my broken bone. Let me say that again—thank You for healing me! I'm so ready to have this cast off. It's been awkward and uncomfortable, and I'm happy that after today I won't have to wear it any more. You have sent people to help me—people such as doctors, nurses, and x-ray technicians. Thank You for them. I know that my health and healing come from You. You created me, You sustain me, and You promise me that one day I will be in heaven with You, where there will be no more broken bones, no more pain, and no more casts. Thank You, Lord! Amen.

Getting Braces Put On—Lord Jesus, I'm a little anxious and a little excited at the same time. Some people have told me that braces hurt, and some people have told me that I'll be glad that I'm getting them. I know that both things are probably true. Today I ask You to help me remember to take good care of my teeth and my braces so they have the greatest benefit. I ask You to bless my orthodontist and staff. I thank You for always being with me, for taking away my sins, and for promising me eternal life with You. Amen.

Getting Braces Taken Off—Lord Jesus, the day to get my braces off is finally here, and I'm very, very thankful! It wasn't always easy to have them on, so I'll be glad to have them off. Help me to remember to take care of my teeth, to follow my orthodontist's directions, and to wear my retainers. Good oral hygiene is one of the ways I can take care of myself, and when I do that, I honor You. Amen.

Getting Glasses—Dear God, the day has come for me to get new glasses. It will be so good to be able to see better. Help me to take good care of my glasses so they don't get lost or broken. Thank You for my eyes, which can see beauty in the world You made. Thank You for my ears and nose and voice. May I use all my body and senses to enjoy the gifts You have given me and to give You praise and glory. In Jesus' name I pray. Amen.

Hymn Stanzas

Praise God, from whom all
 blessings flow;
Praise Him, all creatures here below;
Praise Him above, you heav'nly host:
Praise Father, Son, and Holy Ghost.
Amen.

("Praise God, from Whom All Blessings Flow," *LSB* 805:1)

Lord, take my hand and lead me,
Upon life's way;
Direct, protect, and feed me
From day to day.
Without Your grace and favor
I go astray;
So take my hand, O Savior,
And lead the way.

("Lord, Take My Hand and Lead Me," *LSB* 722:1)

Forth in Thy name, O Lord, I go,
My daily labor to pursue,
Thee, only Thee, resolved to know
In all I think or speak or do.

The task Thy wisdom has assigned,
O let me cheerfully fulfill;
In all my works Thy presence find,
And prove Thy good and perfect will.

For Thee delightfully employ
Whate'er Thy bounteous grace has giv'n,
And run my course with even joy,
And closely walk with Thee to heav'n.

("Forth in Thy Name, O Lord, I Go," *LSB* 854:1–2,5)

Scripture Verses

The LORD bless you and keep you; the LORD make His face to shine upon you and be gracious to you; the LORD lift up His countenance upon you and give you peace.

(Numbers 6:24–26)

Be strong and courageous. Do not fear or be in dread of them, for it is the LORD your God who goes with you. He will not leave you or forsake you.

(Deuteronomy 31:6)

Trust in the LORD with all your heart, and do not lean on your own understanding. In all your ways acknowledge Him, and He will make straight your paths.

(Proverbs 3:5–6)

The LORD will keep you from all evil; He will keep your life. The LORD will keep your going out and your coming in from this time forth and forevermore.

(Psalm 121:7–8)

Fear not, for I am with you; be not dismayed, for I am your God; I will strengthen you, I will help you, I will uphold you with My righteous right hand.

(Isaiah 41:10)

For I know the plans I have for you, declares the LORD, plans for welfare and not for evil, to give you a future and a hope.

(Jeremiah 29:11)

Come to Me, all who labor and are heavy laden, and I will give you rest. Take My yoke upon you, and learn from Me, for I am gentle and lowly in heart, and you will find rest for your souls. For My yoke is easy, and My burden is light.

(Matthew 11:28–30)

Immediately Jesus spoke to them, saying, "Take heart; it is I. Do not be afraid."

(Matthew 14:27)

I have said these things to you, that in Me you may have peace. In the world you will have tribulation. But take heart; I have overcome the world.

(John 16:33)

He has said, "I will never leave you nor forsake you."

(Hebrews 13.5)

The Spirit helps us in our weakness. For we do not know what to pray for as we ought, but the Spirit Himself intercedes for us with groanings too deep for words.

(Romans 8:26)

INDEX